Our Government

Joanne Wachter

We the People
of the United States
insure domestic Tranquility, provide for the common defence, promote the general
and our Posterity, do ordain and establish this Constitution for the United States of
Article I

We have a Constitution.

We have a President.

We have a Congress.

We have a Supreme Court.

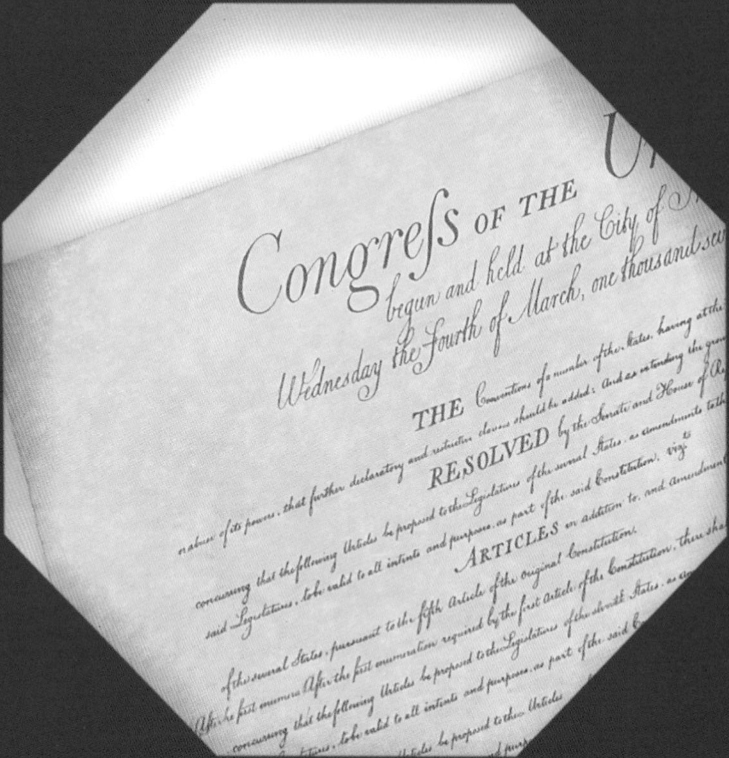
Congress OF THE
begun and held at the City of
Wednesday the Fourth of March, one thousand and
THE
RESOLVED
ARTICLES

We have a Bill of Rights.

We have a history.

I love the U.S.A.!